Step by Step

A Guide to

A Search for God

Book I

GW00568767

A.R.E. PRESS • VIRGINIA BEACH • VIRGINIA

Copyright © 1988
by the
Edgar Cayce Foundation
All rights reserved
ISBN 87604-229-9

Printed in the U.S.A.

2nd Printing, August 1990

CONTENTS

INTRODUCTION

Welcome to a new venture in spiritual growth. You're about to begin an exciting "venture inward." Your road map is a special program of study called *A Search for God,* which was developed from the psychic readings of the American clairvoyant, Edgar Cayce.

This program is one of the most effective learning tools to have come through the work of Edgar Cayce. Meeting in what are actually informal spiritual workshops, people of all ages and from all walks of life make practical use of the concepts presented in the Cayce readings. The source material—*A Search for God,* Books I and II—guides the Study Group through periods of prayer, meditation, reading, and discussion to an increase in self-awareness.

Within each group, members have an opportunity not only to study and discuss, but also to test and to apply the precepts found in the lessons. Working together, individuals create an actual field of mental and spiritual energy which can accelerate their individual growth. Study Groups, therefore, become a laboratory for spiritual research—the results of which become effective in the home, in personal worship, even at the office.

The lessons in *A Search for God* were begun in 1931 by a small group of people interested in Edgar Cayce's psychic gifts. They asked for a reading on how they might help give light and truth to the world! So began a series of readings on spiritual laws. These readings suggested the main subjects of each chapter and provided insights into those subjects. The group members were then instructed to take the principles described and put them into practical application in their daily lives. As the members of this first group tried to live the spiritual laws, they combined the insights from Cayce's readings with their own experiences to write the lessons you'll be studying. When each chapter was finished, the material was reviewed by Edgar Cayce in his altered state of consciousness. It took the members of this Study Group *eleven years* to test the concepts and compile the material in this completed program.

As you meet regularly with other individuals interested in spiritual growth and psychic awareness, you will discover the power of group study. This handbook will make your Study Group activity a more meaningful and rewarding experience. The handbook follows *A Search for God,* Book I, chapter by chapter, providing you with five "tools" to enhance your study:

1. Things to do

This section offers suggestions for applying the principles in your own life. The information in the lessons becomes meaningful only as you *use* it.

2. Things to think

Here is a list of questions, thoughts, and affirmations to ponder as you study the lesson.

3. Things to figure out

This is a collection of hypothetical life situations which relate to the principles in each lesson. You're invited to puzzle over these scenarios individually or as a group.

4. Questions to discuss

These are questions related directly to the material you'll be reading. You're encouraged to use these questions as they're needed to stimulate group discussion in your meetings. These questions will be particularly helpful when it's your turn to lead the group.

5. Suggested supplemental reading

This section offers suggestions for extra reading which may enhance each particular lesson.

Although *A Search for God,* Book I, begins with preliminary information on meditation, Part I of this handbook starts with "Lesson One—Cooperation." Part II contains sections on prayer, meditation, and affirmations which will help you understand the opening pages of *A Search for God,* Book I.

If you're preparing for your group's first meeting, turn to page 75 for your group's next step.

If you're planning to visit a group for the first time, turn to page 92 for *your* next step.

Suggested Meeting Format

MOMENT OF SILENCE

Meetings usually begin with a shared moment of silence and perhaps a short prayer. This helps the group members focus their energies on the special purpose of the next two hours.

WEEKLY DISCIPLINE

Then, the group members take a few minutes to tell what happened during the week as they tried to apply last week's material. Application is the magic word. This is a special part of the meeting. You'll see how people's lives change when they apply spiritual laws.

READING AND DISCUSSION

The group then spends about an hour reading and discussing portions of a chapter from *A Search for God.* These two *A Search for God* books will guide you through a program of psychic and spiritual development which was outlined by Edgar Cayce in a special series of readings. The group discussion often stimulates thinking and leads to new insights into the material. This is a vital part of the Study Group experience. To help generate group discussion, this handbook includes discussion questions for each chapter.

SETTING THE WEEK'S DISCIPLINE

After the discussion period your group selects a specific way to apply this material in daily living. This handbook contains several discipline suggestions for each chapter. At the next meeting you'll report on your results.

MEDITATION AND PRAYER

Next, your group will share in a period of quiet reflection together. This quiet time is called "meditation." If you're not familiar with meditation, just consider this a time of peaceful silence. It will last for 10 to 15 minutes. After the time of quiet, there is a closing prayer which ends the meditation. (A more specific outline for the meditation period can be found in the "When You Meditate as a Group" section on page 86 of Part II.) The meditation period usually ends the meeting. It's important to end on time. People will appreciate punctuality both in beginning and in ending the Study Group meeting.

GROUP NEWS AND LOCAL EVENTS

After the meditation, there is occasionally some informal sharing of mailings of special interest from A.R.E. Headquarters at Virginia Beach or information about local A.R.E. activities. This is also a good time to give a voluntary contribution as described on page 93.

PART I

The
Lessons

LESSON ONE

Cooperation

THINGS TO DO

Choose one of the following and try it for a week:

1. Look for opportunities during the week when you can "go along" with someone else's choice or decision.
2. Each day during the week as you awaken, ask three times, "What would You have me do today?" Then listen. Keep reminding yourself of this during the day and see where it takes you.
3. When faced with decisions during the week, stop and ask yourself, "What would God have me do?"
4. When interacting with a difficult or irritating person, think to yourself, "Lord, he/she is Thine, even as I am Thine. Help me do that which will bring peace and harmony between us." Then act on that thought.
5. Make a concerted effort to refrain from any unkind words (or thoughts) to or about anyone for at least one day during the week. Watch and see what happens that day.
6. Join with the group in agreeing to do one thing this week that will help create a sense of oneness. Some examples:
   Pray for one another.
   Ask for a dream about the group.
   Choose an outside service project.
   Agree on a concern about which all can pray.
   Agree to meditate at the same time.

7. List the things that you believe are necessary for "right living." Circle those that you feel are realistic for you to do at this time. Choose one of those that are reasonable and possible and try to do it for one day.

8. Cooperate with the forces of the universe by numbering slips of paper from 1-7. When it comes time to choose an experiment, place the numbers in a container and pick one at random. Match that number with one of the experiments and try that one for one week.

THINGS TO THINK

1. Remember how you felt when you were in harmony with the universe? Perhaps when you were in love, or when you experienced a beautiful morning, or during a prayer period. Imagine yourself feeling that way and then use that feeling in a difficult situation that you're facing.

2. a. Make an effort to observe yourself in your daily activities—how well do you cooperate with the "outer laws"?
      For example:
      Do I drive within the speed limit?
      Do I arrive at work on time?
      Are my lunch hours often "extended"?
      Do I pay my bills on time?
      Am I often late so that others have to wait for me?
      Are there ways that I "cut corners"?
      Others? _____
   b. Do I cooperate with certain "inner laws"? For example:
      Am I good at keeping my promises?
      Am I trustworthy?
      Do I respect other people's property?
      Am I truthful in my dealings with others?
      Do I find myself taking advantage of other people?
      Others? _____

3. Think of one of your most positive relationships and determine the qualities which make it good. Which of these qualities could be applied in more difficult relationships?

4. Think about "I must lose myself in Him."

THINGS TO FIGURE OUT

1. John tells his wife Mary that he has decided to follow a vegetarian diet during the upcoming month. This is outside their normal eating plan. What can Mary do to put cooperation into action in this situation?
2. You are relatively new in your department. Co-workers eat lunch together daily. Gossip about other departments is the usual topic. What will you do?
3. Nancy is the boss. She frequently hears the people who work for her criticizing someone else's performance in the company. What can she do to foster cooperation?
4. You have a longtime relationship with an individual who frequently visits your city. It is now taken for granted that your guest room is available. Others in your household do not enjoy the visitor's company and even you are beginning to feel imposed upon. What will you do?

QUESTIONS FOR GROUP DISCUSSION

Organized according to sections within the chapter

Introduction

1. How is physical cooperation different from spiritual cooperation?
2. How does nature demonstrate unity, order, and harmony?

Need for Cooperation

3. What adverse thoughts do you, as an individual, deal with and how may you best turn them into something positive?
4. Can we have the "mind of Christ" without being a "Christian"?

Method of Obtaining Cooperation

5. Have you found it true in your own experience that you receive love when you show yourself lovable? If not, why do you suppose?
6. How do you visualize the force of love and harmony in action?

Realization of Cooperation

7. Do you expect love and joy to reign permanently in your heart overnight? Why or why not?

8. How can we keep our hearts singing with all the problems that we have? Why should we be the "happiest of all chosen"? What makes us so special?

SUGGESTED SUPPLEMENTAL READING

1. *Experiments in a Search for God*, "Cooperation"
2. *Library Series*, Volume 16, *Expanded Search for God*, "Cooperation"
3. *Library Series*, Volume 7, *Study Group Readings*, 262-2 — 262-5
4. Circulating Files:

   #014 Co-Creators with God
   #017 Creative Forces:
       Essence of Life
   #144 Here Am I, Use Me
5. Suggested Bible Verses:
   Psalm 27
   Isaiah 6:8
   Matthew 5, 6 & 7
   I Corinthians 12
   I Thessalonians 5:14-28

LESSON TWO

Know Thyself

THINGS TO DO

Choose one of the following and try it for a week:

1. List five of your strengths. During the week, try to use some of these to serve another person or for another's benefit.
2. For at least one day, "stand aside and watch self go by" in your interactions with other people. Become completely aware of your inner reactions in these relationships.
3. Try to relate to others throughout the week as if your God were always present.
4. During the week, take time to write down what you feel would be an ideal day. Be sure to include activities, relationships, places, etc. Be as detailed as possible. You won't have to share this with anyone so you can be as honest and as creative as you like. Take as many pages as necessary to describe as much as you can. Decide on one action that you can do this week to move toward your ideal day. Then seal the pages in an envelope and put it away in a safe place. Sometime in the future, perhaps a year, or five years or even ten years, look at it again to see how many details have manifested.
5. Set aside some time during the week to determine what kind of world into which you want to be born. Choose one of those items and try to help create that kind of world with your thoughts and actions today.
   For example: I would want to be born into a world that was more accepting of differences. What can I do today? Where can I be more accepting?

or

I'd like a world in which there was no tyranny. Where am I being tyrannical over others? Over myself?

or

I'd like a world in which there was a lot more laughter. I'll try to find humor in more situations.

6. Pick one action to do each day for a week that improves your body as a temple of God. This may include a period of exercises, a change in your diet, refraining from a particular habit, or just a moment of rest.

7. Spend the week building positive mental attitudes. Avoid judging or criticizing others. Repeat the following affirmation as you meditate and whenever you feel vulnerable to negative attitudes such as doubt or fear: "My mind is a builder of positive, loving thoughts, which bring me closer to my Creator."

8. Make a list of your goals and desires in life. How do they benefit others? How do they benefit yourself?

9. In your interactions with others throughout the week, keep the Master's words in mind: "As ye do it unto one of the least of these, ye do it unto Me."

10. Ask the group leader to number slips of paper from 1-9. When it comes time to choose an experiment, pass around a container with the numbered slips and have each group member choose one. Match the number with the experiment listed. If it is one that you agree to do, choose it for a week. If you do not think it is appropriate for you at this time, feel free to choose another (or as many as needed) until you get one that you think is yours. Be sure to note your thoughts and feelings as you decide which one is "yours" and use this insight to learn more about yourself and your responses.

THINGS TO THINK

1. Three times each day, repeat this affirmation silently to yourself, "God, help me to be patient with myself and others."

2. Each evening for a week, think back over the day and examine your words and actions. Ask yourself, "Did I express to others my concept of God?"

3. In ancient Greece, people flocked to the oracle at Delphi to seek answers to their questions and concerns. We're told that engraved over the temple that housed the oracle were the

words "Know Thyself." Why do you think this quote is also used as the second chapter in Edgar Cayce's lessons on spiritual and psychic growth? How can knowing ourselves make us more psychic or better able to receive the type of guidance the Greeks sought at Delphi?

THINGS TO FIGURE OUT

1. A department manager with whom you must interact has a very emotional nature and frequently loses his temper. You find yourself trying to avoid interaction which is beginning to hinder your performance. What can you learn about yourself from this situation?
2. You've been trying to alter your diet to include more fruits and vegetables and less desserts and snacks. How can you use your mind to control your physical desires?
3. Jane has been through several relationships. Each has ended with arguments and bad feelings. How can she come to understand the dynamics of this pattern and change it?
4. Tom has a hard time overlooking the faults of others. Their shortcomings anger him and he often finds himself creating inner dialogues where he tells people what's wrong with their personalities. How can Tom resolve his frustration with others?
5. Alex has had a particularly stressful week at work and at home. He is really looking forward to going out for a few drinks with his co-workers on Friday afternoon. Just before quitting time, however, he gets a call from a recently divorced, male friend (a reformed alcoholic) who is emotionally upset and desperately needs someone to talk to tonight. What does Alex do?

QUESTIONS FOR GROUP DISCUSSION

Organized according to sections within the chapter

Introduction

1. If we're to be measured by what we give, let's each take a turn and name two or three talents or resources that we *can* give.

The Physical Body

2. If it takes complete surrender in order to know ourselves, to whom or what must we surrender? What kinds of service can

you think of to go along with prayer and meditation?

The Mental and Spiritual Bodies

3. What does it mean "As a tree falls, so will it lie"?

Self in Relation to Others

4. Each take a turn and recall a time when you helped someone whom you considered a "foe." Discuss how this affected your relationship with the person.

The Awakening of Self

5. How do we know when His Spirit is bearing witness with our spirit?
6. What does it mean to be "sons (children) of God"?

Conclusion

7. How do you understand "realms of other experiences"?

SUGGESTED SUPPLEMENTAL READING

1. *Experiments in a Search for God*, "Know Thyself"
2. *Library Series*, Volume 16, *Expanded Search for God*, "Know Thyself"
3. *Library Series*, Volume 7, *Study Group Readings*, 262-5 — 262-11
4. Circulating Files: #027 First Find Self
                                #143 Know Yourself
5. Suggested Bible Verses: Proverbs 20
                                Luke 6 & 11
                                Romans 12
                                James 1:22-27

LESSON THREE

What Is My Ideal?

THINGS TO DO

Choose one of the following and try it for a week:

1. Divide a sheet of paper into two columns. Above the left column write, "Goal—An idea of what I want to accomplish in life." Above the right column write, "Ideal—Why I want to accomplish this goal." Then list two or three goals and their accompanying ideals.
2. Pick a time when you can sit quietly for several minutes. With your eyes closed, think back on a time when you felt especially close to God. Try to reawaken that feeling. Then allow a word or phrase to enter your mind which expresses this feeling. Jot this down as one expression of your spiritual ideal.
3. Worksheet for setting ideals:
   A. Divide a blank sheet into three columns. Label the first column "Spiritual Ideals," the second column "Mental Ideals," and the third column "Physical Ideals."
   B. Write in the first column your highest spiritual ideal—the word or words that describe what you perceive to be the highest attainment—a standard of perfection which you want to use to measure your actions.
   C. In the second column, under "Mental Ideals," write those mental attitudes which you feel accurately reflect the word you've written in the Spiritual column. For example, if you wrote "Love" in the Spiritual column, you might want to use words like "acceptance" or "kindness" or "forgiveness" in the Mental column.
   D. Finally, in the last column marked "Physical Ideals," list those physical activities which would express the spiritual

and mental ideals you've just listed. For example, if you've written "forgiveness" as a mental ideal, you might list an activity such as: "Say a friendly word to (person's name) who insulted me yesterday."

E. Use this as a worksheet during the week to further identify and refine your ideals. Once they are set, test them by measuring your activities. Notice the moments when you are successful in living your ideals as well as those that could be improved.

EXAMPLE
Sample Ideals Chart

SPIRITUAL IDEAL MENTAL IDEALS PHYSICAL IDEALS

SPIRITUAL IDEAL	MENTAL IDEALS	PHYSICAL IDEALS
LOVE	ACCEPTANCE	Refrain from complaining about things I can't change.
	KINDNESS	Find time to talk to my neighbor who is going through a hard time.
	FORGIVENESS	Say a friendly word to (person's name) who insulted me yesterday.

4. Choose one word which you would want your friends to use in describing your greatest character strength; for example, kindness, compassion, honesty, helpfulness, etc. Then throughout the week, look for that quality in others as you try to practice it yourself. Keep a journal of your thoughts and feelings each day.

5. The Cayce readings affirm that the qualities we admire in others are also qualities that we ourselves possess. For one week, jot down in a small booklet or on a piece of paper the positive qualities you observe in other people. Each evening review the list and beside each entry write down a few ways that you might express this quality more fully in your own life.

6. Identify for yourself one of your daily "roles"; for example, mother, friend, spouse, employee, etc. What is your concept of the ideal model of this role? Find one thing that he/she would do and practice it each day.

7. Take time at some point during the week to imagine what you want to be like in seven years. If you truly applied everything you know and really worked with spiritual discipline, what kind of person can you imagine yourself to be? Try to visualize your new self in seven years. Then write down four or five qualities or attributes that you see yourself having. Decide how you can *begin* today to become this person. You may want to put this list away and refer to it from time to time.

8. Pick one day in the week to observe carefully your actions as you go about your daily routine. In the evening list five to ten individual actions and ask yourself, "In what spirit did I do this?" Describe each act in terms of its "spirit," such as "spirit of helpfulness," "a loving spirit," or "a spirit of camaraderie." Note also those that were negative, such as "spirit of rebellion," "spirit of defensiveness," or "spirit of getting even." When you've finished this list, choose two to work on in the future: a "positive spirit" to magnify and a "negative spirit" to minimize.

THINGS TO THINK

1. Pick one person with whom you are having difficulties. At least once through the week really work with the affirmation: "Let me see in my brother (sister) that I see in Him whom I worship."

2. Think of the three people you admire most. Ask, "What are their ideals that could motivate such exemplary lives?" Remember, "These ideals are present in me as well, or I couldn't recognize them."
3. What do I desire for myself? What do I desire for my relationship with _____?
4. Examine the purposes in several things that you do this week. With each one ask yourself, "What is my purpose in doing this?"
5. Reflect upon yesterday and your contacts with others. Ask, "Did my every word, thought, and deed bring a blessing to those I contacted? Did many of them?"
6. In the affirmation for this chapter, we ask God to "help us in our unbelief." When your belief wavers, use this lesson's affirmation to build greater belief in your ideal.

THINGS TO FIGURE OUT

1. You work for a small corporation. You've been there for five years and want very much to advance to higher responsibilities and pay scales. Your goals are clear, but what are your ideals that have created these goals? What would be "self-centered ideals"? What would be "God-centered ideals"?
2. Jane has low self-esteem. She can easily accept that what she doesn't like in others is a reflection of herself. However, she has trouble believing that what she admires in others is also a part of herself. How can she learn to accept the positive side of this spiritual law?
3. Jim supervises an employee who tends to rationalize unacceptable work; for example, he complains about, "too little time," "too little help," "too small a budget," etc. Jim's ideal is the Golden Rule: he wants to treat his employee as Jim would want to be treated himself. What would you do if you were Jim?
4. Mary's ideal is to see the Christ in everyone. Several months ago her husband of 25 years left her and married another woman. This forced her to find employment, a new home, and a new way of life. Her new life is going well, yet she has trouble applying her ideal toward her former husband and his new wife. How might she resolve this difficulty?

QUESTIONS FOR GROUP DISCUSSION

Organized according to sections within the chapter

Introduction

1. Can you clarify the difference between ideas and ideals?
2. How do you interpret, "Mind is the builder"? How does this relate to ideals?

Ideals Grow with Development

3. Why has your early understanding of God changed to what it is today?
4. Who in your opinion have been the greatest spiritual leaders? What ideals might they have had in common?

The True Ideal

5. We know that the Edgar Cayce readings honored all religions that worship the One God. How can a non-Christian interpret the phrase, "Our ideal must be found in Christ, who is the Way"?
6. Try putting into words what you consider a high spiritual ideal.

Attaining the Ideal

7. We read that once our ideal is set we will have no fear. How can a better understanding of our ideal help us to overcome anxiety?
8. We are told to look for good in everyone, speaking neither evil, harsh, nor unkind words at any time. How realistic is this? What can you do to make this easier?

Conclusion

9. Our ideal will lift us up and cause us to be merciful. What is mercy? What does it mean to be merciful?

Chapter Review Questions

10. Why is it sometimes easier to see qualities or faults in others than it is to see the same traits in ourselves?
11. Would it be possible for two people to be committed to the very same ideal, and yet not be able to get along and have a very difficult relationship?
12. Why do the readings suggest that it is important to establish and work toward our ideals?

SUGGESTED SUPPLEMENTAL READING

1. *Experiments in a Search for God,* "What Is My Ideal?"
2. *Library Series,* Volume 16, *Expanded Search for God,* "What Is My Ideal?"
3. *Library Series,* Volume 7, *Study Group Readings,* 262-11 — 262-16

Circulating File: #045 Importance of Ideals

5. Suggested Bible Verses: Genesis 37-45
            Exodus 20
            Isaiah 28:10 & 13
            Matthew 20
            Luke 10:30-37
            John 4 & 10
            Philippians 2-4

LESSON FOUR

Faith

THINGS TO DO

Choose one of the following and try it for a week:

1. Pick one day and apply faith toward another person whom you may have doubted in the past. Act on that faith, giving the person an opportunity to live up to it.
2. Jot down a few things you already do to strengthen your faith in yourself and others. What kinds of items are they? Worship? Affirmations? Acts of kindness? Take note through the week of when you're using these "faith builders."
3. Confidence comes from what we've seen, faith from what we haven't seen. Describe an area of your life that uses confidence and one that requires faith. Since faith is developed by exercising it, list some specific ways you might increase your faith and try some of them for a week.
4. This chapter tells us that "Through the exercising of faith, we are able to give enlightenment to others." Write down any times in your life when you have helped another person by applying faith. Whenever you feel a lack of faith in a situation, read over that list and let it remind you of the power of true faith which can "remove mountains."
5. Find suggestions for increasing faith listed in the recommended Biblical passages for this chapter. Choose one or two and apply them for one week.
6. Live a line from the chapter on "Faith."
7. How would you explain faith to someone who didn't know the word at all? Take time this week to write a paragraph on your understanding of faith and how it helps you.

THINGS TO THINK

1. True faith is believing there is a purpose for everything that happens to us. Can I recall living through an unpleasant experience, only to realize its purpose much later?

2. Choose one or two areas in your life where you lack confidence. Determine whether this is because of physical limitations (such as strength or training) or because of mental limitations (such as doubt or fear). Think of how you might improve your confidence through acts of faith. Recognize how physical confidence is limited, whereas true faith knows no bounds.

3. In what ways can I use my mind to strengthen my faith?

4. During World War II, a man seeking information about his son who was missing in action was told in a Cayce reading, "Keep that faith which prompted thee. Let nothing take it from thee. For as you have known, there is nothing in heaven or in hell that may separate thee from the love of God, but thine own self . . . " (5369-2) When faced with a difficult situation, use this affirmation to increase your faith.

5. Often we find that we have faith in some areas but not in others. For example, we may have faith in health matters but not in financial concerns. Think of those areas in which you find faith coming easier. Ask yourself, "Is there some basis for this in my past experience? Religious training? Family background? Other reasons?"

6. Ponder this statement: "It isn't what I profess to believe but the way I live that counts."

7. Faith is not belief without question, but trust without reservation.

THINGS TO FIGURE OUT

1. Because of unforeseen medical bills, the Smiths are very worried. Up until recently, Greg and Val have managed their finances on a very tight budget, since Val only makes a small salary. Greg just found out that, due to budget cuts, he will be out of a job in two weeks. A well-meaning friend offers Greg a job with his company, even though it does not really involve the kind of work that Greg enjoys or for which he is well suited. Greg is torn between taking a job that he doesn't really want for the sake of making ends meet and holding out for

something that will use his abilities. Should he take a chance on waiting for the "right job" to appear in the near future or grab onto what is offered to him right now?
2. John tries to have faith in other people, but he's often disappointed by their actions. He has trouble having faith in God when people have so often let him down. What can he do to increase his faith in God?
3. Joan has always had faith that God would protect those she loves. However, she wonders whether God would really help her get a new job or find her a new place to live. Should she have faith that God would provide these things if needed?
4. Jim has been through some very hard times. He's better now, but he still holds a lot of resentment about experiences that happened to him in the past. How can he use faith to help him heal his bitterness and build a new life?

QUESTIONS FOR GROUP DISCUSSION

Organized according to sections within the chapter
What Is Faith?
1. Is it an act of faith to spend as if we have lots of money and not worry about budgeting? Why or why not?
Need of Faith
2. If faith is victory, can we then use faith to get anything we want? Money? Power over others? What kind of victory does faith provide?
3. Why is our development in direct proportion to our faith in God, in others, and in ourselves?
4. How can having little or no faith in ourselves or in our abilities have an adverse effect on our own spiritual development?
How Faith Is Developed
5. Where in your life can you exercise greater faith?
6. How can your faith be an enlightenment to others?
Where Faith Abounds
7. We know that the Edgar Cayce readings are universal and were given to people of all religions. Discuss how a non-Christian might interpret the word *Master* as it relates to Jesus the Christ.

Self-Analysis Necessary

8. Is it appropriate to pray to God for material things as well as for "peace in mind and soul"? What's the right balance for these two desires?

Evidences of Faith

9. In faith we know that "His promises are sure." What are some of His promises?

Reward of Faith

10. What are some examples of "rewards of faith"?
11. Why are rewards in direct proportion to our faith?

Chapter Review Questions

12. We're told in an Edgar Cayce reading that, "If you would invite confidence, ye must give it. If ye would invite love, ye must show it. If ye would invite faith, ye must show it." (1151-4) Discuss how you might show and express faith in everyday ways; for example, at home, at work.
13. Describe what it is about "the faith of a little child" that makes it a desirable trait.
14. Is there a difference between spiritual faith and religious dogma?
15. There is always a place for faith regardless of whether something is about to happen, is happening now, or has already happened in the past. The following Biblical passages give us illustrations for discussion: Genesis 22:1-18
Matthew 9:18-25
Matthew 14:25-31

SUGGESTED SUPPLEMENTAL READING

1. *Experiments in a Search for God,* "Faith"
2. *Library Series,* Volume 16, *Expanded Search for God,* "Faith"
3. *Library Series,* Volume 7, *Study Group Readings,* 262-17 — 262-18
4. Circulating Files: #149 If You Call, I Will Hear
#005 Anger, Confusion, and Doubt
5. Suggested Bible Verses Exodus 3 & 4
Matthew 17
Luke 12
Hebrews 11

LESSON FIVE

Virtue and Understanding

THINGS TO DO

Choose one of the following and try it for a week:

1. For one day try to focus solely on "whatever things are good."
2. The text defines *virtue* as being "true to what is pure in our purpose."
   A. Choose an activity of interest in your life that reflects your highest purpose.
   B. Write in a sentence or two why you're involved with this activity. (This expresses your "purpose.")
   C. Then spend a week looking for ways to be true to that purpose.
   Example: a. Your activity is making music.
            b. Your purpose in music is to inspire others.
            c. Look for opportunities throughout the week to inspire others in whatever way possible.
3. Choose one action that you believe is "pure in purpose." For one day try expressing this action as much as possible and see what the day brings.
4. For one week set aside a definite time and place that you will be able to work consistently with prayer and meditation. Keep track of both the excuses you find not to keep this time, as well as those reasons that come to mind why you're glad to have this special time set aside. Keep faithful to your commitment throughout the week, nonetheless.
5. Choose one day and practice "emphasizing virtues, minimizing faults" in yourself and in others.

6. Try to spend a day without finding fault with anything or anyone (including yourself).
7. To magnify virtues in a difficult relationship, use the following prayer daily, "Lord, he is Thine, even as I am Thine. Do that which will bring peace and harmony between us."
8. Remember the phrase in the text which says, "Virtue is a shield of protection." During the week, when you feel threatened or discouraged, focus on that phrase.

THINGS TO THINK

1. Each thought and act adds its vibration to my development. What sort of "house" am I building in my daily thoughts and actions?
2. What have I always considered to be "virtuous"? Do I have a different perspective now that I've studied this chapter?
3. Can I remember a time in my life when understanding came as a result of being true to my purpose?
4. Looking back, can I see where "knowledge which was out of harmony with my ideal" became a barrier?
5. Choose an individual whose behavior irritates you. Try to identify an essence of virtue beneath even that irritating behavior.
   Example: Someone is bossy and critical.
   Possible underlying virtue: "A high standard of excellence."
   Use this to understand better that person as a child of God.
6. Throughout the week become aware of all those moments when you feel particularly attuned to spirit or to the Creative Forces around you. Take note of what you were doing or thinking that may have helped you reach this "attunement."
7. At the end of the day, think about any interactions with others that were less than ideal. Ask, "How might I have acted differently in order to express the very best that is within me?"
8. Have I really been true to my commitment to such spiritual disciplines as prayer and meditation?

THINGS TO FIGURE OUT

1. John is very committed to the spiritual path. He wants to make as much progress as possible. He smokes and wonders if this will hinder his spiritual development. He's received

conflicting advice on this question. If he should ask your advice, what would you tell him?

2. Mary is a perfectionist. She has very high standards of conduct and does her very best to live up to them. She feels good about her own behavior. However, her husband's many shortcomings have become a constant source of irritation for her. What can she do?

3. Sally does a good job of seeing the positive qualities in others. However, when she is driving in traffic, she's very critical of other drivers. She says she can't understand how people can be so inconsiderate of others on the road. Lately things have been getting worse and she finds herself screaming and swearing often at other drivers while she's driving. She wants to change, but she's not sure how. What would you suggest she do?

4. George has always found it easy to take care of others. However, he has a problem when it comes to taking care of himself. Somehow he feels it's selfish to spend a lot of thought and energy on himself. He came from a large family where, as the oldest, he always had to watch out for "the younger kids" and help his mother who worked hard caring for everyone. How can George see the virtue in focusing on his own needs?

5. David, a member of a Study Group, has become well versed in his knowledge of spiritual material. It is apparent, however, from his superior attitude and his criticism of others that his knowledge has not given him understanding. How can his Study Group help him?

6. Bill is very dissatisfied with his job. He doesn't agree with the plans and directions the company is taking, and he doesn't believe his boss even listens to his ideas. How can he apply the principles in this chapter to his situation?

QUESTIONS FOR GROUP DISCUSSION

Organized according to sections within the chapter

Introduction

1. How are the definitions of "virtue" and "understanding" different in the text from the typical definitions?

2. How would I describe "purity"? What does it mean to be "pure"?

3. Share with one another those things that you've found help-ful in "keeping yourself in tune with Creative Forces." Choose one new activity that you learn from the discussion and try it every day for a week.
4. How is knowledge different from understanding?
5. How can we discern the difference between holding fast to a purpose that we just feel strongly about and holding fast to one that genuinely originates at a soul level?

Virtue and Understanding Are Spiritual

6. If the desire for virtue and understanding is already within, how do we become more aware of it and enhance it?
7. The text says that "He was tempted but was without sin." From a spiritual perspective, what might be the ingredient that separates "temptation" from "sin"?

Virtue and Understanding Are Essential to Right Living

8. How does going through a difficult experience give you a bet-ter understanding of others?
9. Can you name a time when a good deed done by you didn't seem to have an effect immediately but instead "bore fruit" sometime later?

The Way to Virtue and Understanding

10. What does it mean to be "pure in heart, mind, body, and soul"? Are physical appetites impure?
11. How can we know what God wills for us?

Personal Experience

12. How can we have "faith in the perfection of others" when we so easily see their faults?
13. Where do we need to place our faith? In our God? In our-selves? In our brother?

Virtue Is a Defense, Understanding Is a Weapon

14. What kind of protection does virtue provide?

The Effects of Virtue and Understanding on Ourselves and Others

15. Have you ever "caught the spirit" of love, mercy, justice, patience, or forgiveness through another's example? Share it with the group.

16. This section tells us that "we know we have passed from death unto life because we love." Explain what it means by "death" and "life" in this context.

SUGGESTED SUPPLEMENTAL READING

1. *Experiments in a Search for God,* "Virtue and Understanding"
2. *Library Series,* Volume 16, *Expanded Search for God,* "Virtue and Understanding"
3. *Library Series,* Volume 7, *Study Group Readings,* 262-18 — 262-21
4. Circulating Files: #054 Knowledge: Use and Misuse
   #141 Magnify Agreements, Minimize Differences
5. Suggested Bible Verses: Isaiah 1:10-17
   Proverbs 8-11
   Matthew 6
   Matthew 7
   Romans 14:1-14
   I Corinthians 13
   Galatians 6:1-10
   James 1 & 2

LESSON SIX

Fellowship

THINGS TO DO

Choose one of the following and try it for a week:

1. For one day, pretend that everyone you meet is a beloved member of your family and then treat each person as such.
2. Take time out during the week to enjoy the company of friends. Do something special which brings friends together in a joyful celebration.
3. "There is no better place to practice brotherly love than in the home." Find ways to express love to others in your home: helping with daily chores, being patient, saying words of encouragement. Do you find any change in your home life as a result of these actions?
4. Choose one person who irritates you. Each day for a week, pray to see the Divine in that person. Then do your best throughout the week to really see the best in him or her.
5. Choose a social concern; for example, the homeless, hunger, care of the elderly, etc. Spend a week gathering information about this topic (reading articles or talking to people). Report to the group what you discovered.

or

5a. Actually take part in a community service activity which will bring you into contact with a greater cross-section of people; for example, volunteering in a hospital or soup kitchen, reading to the blind, helping out in a nursing home.
6. For one week, simply keep in mind and try to practice the Golden Rule: Treat others as you would have them treat you.

7. Select a painful or unpleasant situation in your life—currently or in the past—where you have trouble forgiving another person. Each day for a month, pray for help in forgiving this person (and yourself). Then try to release any negative feelings that you carry about this situation by trusting in help from God.

8. Keeping in mind that acts of kindness bring you into a closer fellowship with God, make a concerted effort for one week to practice "kindness and consideration" toward everyone you meet.

THINGS TO THINK

1. According to this chapter, our relationship with others is a reflection of our relationship with God. Think about all the different people that are a part of your day, such as waitresses, janitors, bosses, neighbors, etc. Ask, "What do my attitudes toward these people tell me about my relationship with God?"

2. Repeat this affirmation to yourself as you interact with others during the week: "The way I treat this person is the way I'm treating God."

3. How might the question "Am I my brother's keeper?" assist me in my interactions with others throughout the day?

4. How might I react differently to a particular personality problem or an individual's shortcoming, if I suddenly noticed that same problem in someone I *truly* loved and respected?

5. Throughout the day ponder this thought, "No one can have too many friends."

THINGS TO FIGURE OUT

1. Mary loves her church. She goes to service every Sunday and volunteers for many church projects. However, one thing disturbs her. Although she approves of charity programs, she gets annoyed at the many people who come to the church asking for handouts. Sometimes she sees them as loafers who are taking advantage of the church's goodwill. What would you tell her if she asked your advice on how she can change her attitude?

2. Last year Bob's company hired a new man into a position equal to his. The two of them share many responsibilities. The trouble is that this new employee seems to try deliberately to

make Bob look bad. At first Bob rationalized the evidence, refusing to believe there was any intended malice. However, he's now convinced that this new man (for whatever reason) is determined to damage Bob's reputation. Bob is in a Study Group and is reading the "Fellowship" chapter. It tells him to love his enemies. How can he apply this advice in his situation?

3. Sara and Alice have been friends for many years and their children enjoy one another's company as well. However, Alice has been making malicious remarks to a mutual friend about Sara's abilities as a parent. Now Alice is suggesting that Sara and her children join Alice's family for an outing to the zoo. How should Sara approach the situation?

4. Carol has an acquaintance at work that she doesn't like at all. The person has never done anything mean to her or said anything cruel. In fact, this woman treats her nicely, but Carol just doesn't like her. Why might Carol feel this way? If you were Carol, what would you do?

QUESTIONS FOR GROUP DISCUSSION
Organized according to sections within the chapter
Introduction

1. What is the difference between "Fellowship" and "Brotherhood" as the words are used in this text?
2. How does expressing brotherly love to another increase our fellowship with our God?

Am I My Brother's Keeper?

3. How can loving others empower them to realize their own strength?

Our Fellowship with God

4. How do our thoughts bind others when we dislike or judge them?
5. How is it possible that our fellowship with our God may be found in our understanding of our fellow man?

Fellowship with God, the Need of the World

6. This section promises that "in the most terrible acts" we can see the power of good misdirected. Can you think of examples?
7. If we became truly *aware* of the fact that our every thought,

word, and deed could retard the development of another, how might we act differently tomorrow?

Duty of Those Who Have Fellowship with the Father

8. What do you think is the meaning of Jesus' words, "Ye have not chosen me, but I have chosen you"? Why do you think this is the opening line of this section?

9. Do you think it is our duty not to complain about conditions in our life? Why or why not?

10. How can we begin to interact with others in such a manner that they see the good within us and thus glorify God?

Fellowship Brings a Peace That Passes Understanding

11. By being kind to others do we guarantee kind treatment in return? If not, what's the point in being kind?

SUGGESTED SUPPLEMENTAL READING

1. *Experiments in a Search for God,* "Fellowship"
2. *Library Series,* Volume 16, *Expanded Search for God,* "Fellowship"
3. *Library Series,* Volume 7, *Study Group Readings,* 262-22 — 262-24
4. Circulating Files:

   On Human Relations: #037, #039, #040, #041, #134
   On Friendship: #030

5. Suggested Bible Verses:

   Genesis 4
   Leviticus 26:1-13
   Deuteronomy 30
   Psalm 23
   Matthew 7:1-12
   Matthew 25:31-45
   Luke 6:27-49
   Luke 19:1-10
   I John 1:1-10

LESSON SEVEN

Patience

THINGS TO DO

Choose one of the following and try it for a week:

1. Each day for a week seek to live more in the present moment by reminding yourself, "Be here now."
2. We are told that perfect attunement with our ideal is necessary for developing patience. For one week, commit to an extra prayer time during which you ask for help in living your ideal.
3. For one day: "Let us live just today, as if the race were ended, the work completed—as if upon this day's endeavors depended the fulfillment of all of His promises."
4. Think of a person or situation which often tries your patience. For one week consider this a special opportunity to exercise more patience. Work at being constructive in thoughts, words, acts, and pray for understanding of the other person's point of view. Take note how this discipline affects your attitudes.
5. For a week greet each experience with the affirmation: "Thank You, God, for giving me just what I need at this time."
6. Patience is the reward for learning to see God in everyone. Spend the week looking for the spark of God in every person you meet.
7. Spend one day as if you were preparing for a visit from God. What changes would you make in attitude or action?

8. Each morning, think about one situation that might occur during the day where you intend to act with patience. Follow through with your intent.

9. Throughout the week, be aware of those around you who express patience in difficult circumstances. Notice how others respond. How do you think their patience changes the outcome of the situation?

10. The next time you start to lose your patience, perform some physical action (such as counting to 10 or closing your thumb to your middle finger) which can give you a few seconds to redirect your thoughts and energies.

THINGS TO THINK

1. Ponder this concept from the readings: Patience is becoming aware of that which is the impelling influence in my experience.

2. Keep in mind that "We are building for eternity." Try to see your daily experiences in the perspective of this long-range view.

3. Consider this, "I cannot change the past. However, I can change how I respond to what is happening to me now and thus affect the future."

4. Recall something you worried about in the past. Ask yourself, "Can I see now that it somehow worked out for the good?"

5. Consider how much patience God must have with us. Does this make it easier to be patient with others?

6. Remember to be patient with yourself as well as with others. When you fail at a discipline or a task, forgive yourself and try again.

7. Consider how this aphorism applies to the chapter: "What the caterpillar calls the end of the world, the wise soul calls a butterfly."

THINGS TO FIGURE OUT

1. Lately Janet has been going through some hard times. Her husband has lost his job and has become very difficult to live with. Janet has also developed some medical problems which concern her. What insights from this chapter could Janet use to get through this difficult time?

2. John works for a small advertising firm. Much of his job in-

volves brainstorming ideas with the rest of the staff. Many of the other staff members very aggressively promote their own opinions while often disregarding or even ridiculing his. Up to now John has allowed this to continue, thinking he was practicing the virtue of patience. Now that John's Study Group is on the "Patience" chapter and his understanding of patience has changed, he's confused about what to do in this situation. He's asked for your help. What would you advise him?

3. Here are two examples of how different people handled similar experiences:

   a. Mark makes his living as a construction worker but has a strong side interest in computers. Recently he had a serious fall at work and broke his leg. He knew he would be unable to return to work for several months. Since he is an active person, Mark decided to take advantage of this period of inactivity by attending computer classes at his local community college.

   b. Marie's career as a dancer with a well-known ballet company was just starting to progress when she and her husband learned that she was expecting a baby. They are both happy about the news since they want a family. However, Marie is feeling extremely frustrated and impatient with this sudden halt to her career. She figures that the only thing she can do is sit around and patiently wait out the pregnancy. Once the baby arrives and a babysitter is hired, Marie can get on with her career.

   What is the difference between active and passive patience? How can Marie express active patience in her situation?

QUESTIONS FOR GROUP DISCUSSION

Organized according to sections within the chapter

Introduction

1. Why is patience so crucial to "knowing self," "measuring and testing ideals," "using faith," and "seeking understanding through virtue"?

2. How can patience put virtue into action?

Value of Patience

3. What is the "pearl of great price" that is won through patience?

4. Can you think of a person whose life shines with the beauty of patience? What is it about that person that is special?

Means Through Which Patience Is Gained

5. Does patience mean always allowing others to dominate you? If not, what else could it mean?
6. How can patience be "an active growing force" rather than "passive submission"?
7. According to this chapter, "We are not called upon to live what we do not understand." How do you interpret this?
8. Why does selfishness retard our progress in gaining patience?

It Takes Patience to Run the Race

9. What are the "influences within" that "are stronger than from without"?

Personal Experiences

10. Why is patience the "watch at the gateway leading from the physical body to the soul"?
11. Explain, "In patience possess ye your souls!"

SUGGESTED SUPPLEMENTAL READING

1. *Library Series,* Volume 16, *Expanded Search for God,* "Patience"
2. *Experiments in a Search for God,* "Patience"
3. *Library Series,* Volume 7, *Study Group Readings,* 262-25 — 262-27
4. *Library Series,* Volume 15, *Attitudes and Emotions,* "Patience"

5. Circulating Files: #125 Time, Space, Patience
   #086 Patience and Problems

6. Suggested Bible Verses: Psalm 73
   Isaiah 11 & 12
   Lamentations 3:22-36
   Matthew 5:1-12
   Luke 8:5-18
   Luke 21:19
   Romans 5:1-8
   Hebrews 12:1-2
   James 1:1-12
   II Peter 1:1-8

LESSON EIGHT

The Open Door

THINGS TO DO

Choose one of the following and try it for a week:

1. Each day for a week, try to bring a moment of happiness or joy into someone's day. This may be as simple as a smile or a kind word.
2. Spend one week relating to others with the attitude, "I am an open door through which God is working. Let me remain open."
3. For one day make every effort to "manifest in love" all that you do in your daily activities. See where the day takes you.
4. Decide for yourself what "losing self in Him" means and then attempt to live it one day during the week in just that manner.
5. When trying to make a decision, ask "What would God have me do?" Then try to act or think according to how you answer that question.
6. Interpret for yourself this passage and apply it for one week, "Let us choose each day some truth, live it first for self, then for others . . . "
7. This week, look for opportunities to serve someone outside your normal circle of family and friends.
8. Set aside an additional time for special meditation to be aware of the Christ Consciousness within you.
9. Practice for one week: "When doubts arise, it is a call to prayer."
10. For one week make a conscious effort to put someone else's good or need before your own.

11. Try to minimize any thoughts of doubt, lack, or self-condemnation.
12. When feeling troubled or discouraged, try drawing on the "force, power, and activity" offered to you by the Christ Spirit or God.
13. Try to feel the reality of "I and my Father are one."

THINGS TO THINK

1. This week, take time at the end of each day to reflect on those instances where the Christ Spirit was magnified in someone else or in a particular action.
2. Remember that "those we meet along the way are seekers also."
3. How do I experience God? (For example, is God an arbitrary master? an all-wise provider? a loving Father or Mother? etc.)
4. For one week, review each day to see whether your thoughts and activities did or did not reflect "His Spirit."
5. Ponder this thought: By our acts, words, and deeds we have chosen to receive as we have given, to be measured as we measure and to be forgiven as we forgive.
6. What are my reasons for wanting to become a more perfect channel of God's activities in the earth?
7. Ponder this: "In application comes awareness."
8. Am I able to appreciate "another's good" as well as my own? Can I appreciate my *own* good as well as another's?

THINGS TO FIGURE OUT

1. Susan and Dave have been very involved in metaphysical studies for about a year. At first they maintained a great deal of enthusiasm for their meditation and spiritual disciplines. Lately, however, they've been plagued with a series of financial setbacks which have left them full of anxiety about money and other material concerns. This situation seems to have affected their spiritual studies. They have trouble meditating, reading, or applying spiritual principles. What's worse, they're beginning to feel cheated in life and have a growing anger toward those who seem to have unfair advantages. What would you do if you were in their situation?
2. John wants to live up to his spiritual ideals. He has read that service is a very necessary element to spiritual growth. There-

fore, John has enthusiastically sought out opportunities to serve others. Last month, he volunteered to teach eighth-grade Sunday school for his church. With every good intention he attempted to share with the kids his new-found insights into spirituality. To his dismay, the students preferred to carry on their own conversations. They largely ignored him and even ridiculed his attempts at restoring order. He has continued with this commitment for four weeks, and each Sunday has been the same. Now John is perplexed and a bit irritated. He has offered his service as he felt he should, but feels unappreciated and even rejected. What can John learn from this episode concerning service?

3. Margaret has been attending her Search for God group regularly for many months. She knows that she wants to continue and that it has been helpful for her. As the group studied "The Open Door," she felt increasing dismay and disappointment. She had never experienced the "still small voice" and now feels that she is failing to achieve spiritual growth. She has confided her feelings and concerns to you. What will you say?

QUESTIONS FOR GROUP DISCUSSION
Organized according to sections within the chapter

Introduction

1. This chapter states that oneness is the destiny of every soul. Do you think this means that *all* souls will eventually reach this state? What if a soul doesn't try?
2. If the "kingdom of God" is every soul's destiny, why didn't God just send us there to begin with?
3. Each of the previous lessons has emphasized a particular attribute of the soul. How have the seven lessons studied so far raised your consciousness concerning Christ-like action?

The Preparation of Self

4. We're told to "obliterate all selfish thoughts" in order to open the door, but what is "selfish"? Are material concerns, such as having enough money to pay the bills or protecting your belongings, selfish?
5. Why are both "faith" and "good works" (service) important for becoming a channel of spiritual activity in the earth?
6. How do selfishness and oversensitvity prevent us from acting according to our ideals?

How to Open the Door

7. What does it mean to "name the Name"?

8. Why do you think being of service to another person causes the Christ Spirit to enter into our lives?

How to Know the Father

9. Do you agree that it's important to let individuals experience the necessary stages of their own development? Can you give an example?

10. Discuss one occasion when you felt close to God simply by being of service to another person.

The Great Need for Service

11. This section advises us to act so that "others may see our good works as we put into practical operation just what we say we believe and teach." How can we do this without becoming self-important?

12. Why do you think that it's important to demonstrate in our lives what we would teach others?

13. "Man is considering his relationship with his fellow man as never before." Do you see evidence around you that will either support or refute this statement?

The Kingdom of the Father

14. How does this section recommend that we handle doubt?

Chapter Review Questions

15. Discuss this definition of "the Christ Consciousness" as understood through the Edgar Cayce readings:

> The awareness of the soul's oneness with God—written as a pattern on the mind and waiting to be awakened by the will.

SUGGESTED SUPPLEMENTAL READING

1. *Experiments in a Search for God,* "The Open Door"
2. *Library Series,* Volume 16, *Expanded Search for God,* "The Open Door"
3. *Library Series,* Volume 7, *Study Group Readings,* 262-28 — 262-31
4. *Library Series,* Volume 11, *Christ Consciousness*

5. Circulating Files:

#012 Christ Consciousness
#118 Spirit Is the Life, Mind
Is the Builder, Physical Is
the Result

6. Suggested Bible Verses:

Leviticus 26:11-13
I Kings 19:9-12
Jeremiah 1:17-19
Jeremiah 30:22
Matthew 5:3-48
Mark 10
Luke 17:11-23
Galatians 2:19-21
Hebrews 8:10
Revelation 3:20-22

In His Presence

THINGS TO DO

Choose one of the following and try it for a week:

1. We are encouraged to be on speaking terms with God. This week, take time within each day to pause and converse with God, sharing your thoughts and feelings.
2. For one week make every effort to "sense the presence of God within and without."
3. For one week make a special point in your meditation to "listen" for the still, small voice.
4. Read or recite the 23rd Psalm every day, keeping in mind that this is God's promise to you today.
5. Make a list of what are for you the "laws of righteous judgment and clean living." Then for one week, try to live by those laws.
6. Make a special practice for a week to serve another through "kind words, thoughts, and deeds."
7. Make a special effort to get out into nature. Look at the beauty of trees, stars, and flowers. Try to see all of these as living aspects of the Maker. Let this perspective bring to you an increased sense of the abiding presence of a loving God.
8. Watch what thoughts and activities fill your free time. What do you think about most during your moments of leisure?
9. Throughout the day, say silently within to each person you contact, "I acknowledge the spirit of God in you." How does this affect your attitudes?
10. Decide on a specific thing you can do this week that will help bring greater harmony to your physical body.

11. During the week trust in the promise that "God's abiding presence is shadowing and protecting you."
12. Think of a situation in which you've "done all that you know to do." Set aside a special time every day to pray for guidance on the next step.
13. Each day for a week try to experience the phrase, "His spirit bears witness with my spirit."

THINGS TO THINK

1. How personal is my relationship to God?
2. We're told that our physical surroundings reflect our understanding of God. Mentally examine each room in your house. Which one needs to be cleaned or improved? Ask, "Can this room possibly symbolize an area of my life that needs attention?"
3. Do I meditate more in "good times" or in "bad times"? Do I pray and meditate because I want to or because I think I should?
4. How often can I really feel the loving and abiding presence of God? What can I do to feel it more consistently?
5. Am I comfortable with the idea that the Divine dwells in my body and mind?
6. Think on this excerpt from an Edgar Cayce reading: " . . . He *is* that friend that would ever guide, direct and *accompany* thee, in trials, temptations, in thy joys as well as sorrows." (1173-10)
7. "The Lord is my shepherd." What does that really mean to me?

THINGS TO FIGURE OUT

1. Bob has worked in advertising for five years. For most of that time he has done paperwork quietly at his desk. However, he's recently been promoted to a position in which he must present his ideas to prospective clients. He immediately discovered that these presentations terrify him. He doesn't know what to do. He doesn't want to lose his new position, yet in order to continue he must overcome this fear. What could you suggest from the chapter "In His Presence" that might help him?
2. Peter has recently been transferred by his company to a new city. He enjoys his job but is having problems adjusting to his

new environment. He has tried to make friends with his co-workers but they think he is weird and foolish because he is interested in spiritual development and meditates regularly. More and more, Peter is feeling that he just doesn't "belong." Although he realizes that God is always with him, the sense of isolation and fear is almost overwhelming at times. What can Peter do to reinforce the realization of God's presence with him and others in this situation?

3. Joan's husband was just laid off at the factory. They have two small children and very little savings. Joan doubts he will be able to find work easily and admits to her Study Group that she is afraid and asks for help. She'd really like some specific suggestions from the group about how they have overcome fear and doubt in their own experiences so that she can help both herself and her husband. What would you tell her?

4. Joe is the owner of a small store. Daily he works very closely with his clerks. He has tried hard to apply the lessons from *A Search for God* in his relationships with his employees. However, one night driving home he realizes he feels very unappreciated. He seems to be always the one who gives the pat on the back or the smile or says the kind word. He feels very much in need of some caring and concern. How might the information in this chapter help Joe understand these feelings?

QUESTIONS FOR GROUP DISCUSSION

Organized according to sections within the chapter

Introduction

1. What are some of the ways we may experience the "still, small voice within"?

The Knowledge of His Presence

2. The text promises that "He will withhold no good thing from those who seek Him, who seek to do His will." Is this a promise of material rewards for loving God? What is *your* understanding of the promise here?

The Preparation of Self

3. What might be an example of the "breaking up of the carnal forces"?

Experiencing the Abiding Presence

4. How can you be "joyful in service" when it requires "great sacrifice"?

Personal Experiences

5. Do you agree that we should be an "advertisement for God"?

Let Us Remember That Our Guard Is Ever in His Presence

6. Why might mental power alone become a hindrance?

Chapter Review Questions

7. How can we keep from resenting those who seem to be leading others in a direction opposite from our understanding of God's teachings?

8. What do we need to feed our spiritual nature, and how do we get it?

SUGGESTED SUPPLEMENTAL READING

1. *Experiments in a Search for God,* "In His Presence"
2. *Library Series,* Volume 16, *Expanded Search for God,* "In His Presence"
3. *Library Series,* Volume 7, *Study Group Readings,* 262-32 — 262-34
4. Circulating Files:
   #107 Serving in Accord with Ideals
   #145 Kingdom of Heaven Is Within
   #149 If You Call, I Will Hear
5. Suggested Bible Verses:
   Deuteronomy 6:4-13
   Psalm 23
   Psalm 91
   Psalm 139:1-10
   Matthew 25:31-40
   Luke 11:5-13
   John 14-17
   I Corinthians 11:23-25
   Philippians 2:5-18

The Cross
and the Crown

THINGS TO DO

Choose one of the following and try it for a week:

1. Jesus accepted His cross and through that acceptance overcame it. Throughout the week, try to accept what happens to you as a way of moving toward the law of grace.
2. The message Jesus proclaimed from the cross was "Forgive them." Try to apply this ideal of forgiveness for one week, as you trust in the Spirit to give you strength.
3. For a week be especially aware of the crosses borne by others. "Take on their crosses" by feeling compassion and empathy for their situations. Then pray for them, offering yourself in service as you are called.
4. For one day practice being joyful in any situation that normally seems burdensome. Perhaps just smiling or humming an upbeat tune will be enough to turn the circumstances around. You might also try visualizing something pleasant whenever you know you will be encountering someone or experiencing something negative.
5. For one week choose the ideal of "long-suffering," which actually refers to patient and determined endurance. See if manifesting patience, both with yourself and with those around you, makes you more able to bear the stresses of your life.
6. For one week notice whether or not your own difficulties seem easier to deal with when you're being of service to someone else.

7. For one day truly practice all that you believe. If the opportunity arises to "preach" to someone else try to do it through example rather than verbally.

8. For a week, try living a life of total "faith-ful-ness."

9. Look for opportunities throughout the week to "bring spiritual harmony into physical vibration." Each day make note of one example of how you were able to do this.

10. Pretend you're explaining this chapter to a non-Christian. Rather than focusing on the specifics of the Christian faith, try to specify two or three universal ideals that are demonstrated in the life and teachings of Jesus. Choose one of these ideals and try to express it daily for a week.

THINGS TO THINK

1. What would it feel like to have an awareness of His force, His power, and His activity in every avenue of my life?

2. This chapter promises that the key to overcoming crosses is to "keep on keeping on." Some have found the use of affirmations to be helpful in these situations. "This is an experience, let's get through it" and "This too shall pass" are two examples of such affirmations. Which one would you find helpful?

3. Identify two or three activities or experiences in your week that you really look forward to. Determine why you enjoy these so much. Ask yourself, "Are others also benefiting from these moments?"

4. Reflect on why Jesus took the path of the cross. What do you think were His purposes, desires, motivations?

5. In what ways are my actions examples of "Him walking with me day by day"?

6. What material or carnal influences in my life am I hesitant to discard? Why is this so?

7. What aspects of my life may be responsible for limiting the full expression of my inner self?

8. Which "spiritual attribute" presented in the earlier chapters is the hardest for me to apply in my daily life? Why is it so hard for me?

9. Ponder this question from the lesson: "Why must I, as a soul in a material plane, bear a cross?"

THINGS TO FIGURE OUT

1. Michael has had a very devastating year. First, he suffered through a painful divorce which left him emotionally exhausted. Secondly, as a result, he has come down with a serious illness which may force him to quit his job. This would leave him in financial ruin. He is in your Study Group and has asked for help in understanding and healing his situation. Some of the other members have insisted that his suffering is of his own making. They suggest that he search his soul to find out why he is causing himself to suffer. Are these people responding to Michael's plight in an appropriate way? What will you say to Michael when he asks for your counsel?

2. Anita has often gone out of her way to help someone in the neighborhood. She's taken care of neighbors' children at the last minute "as a favor," dropping her own plans in the process. She's often relied upon for a "quick ride" to the store when someone else's car isn't available or the person is unable to drive. At the office she consistently helps others on projects that frequently have nothing to do with her own job. Because of this, she sometimes has had to take her own work home to keep from falling behind. She's truly trying to be of service to everyone and yet she sometimes feels that her good nature allows her to be taken advantage of by others. What can she do?

3. Margaret's baby died shortly after birth. She and her husband had been especially excited about the pregnancy because she'd been feeling somewhat restless and discontent. She thought maybe a new baby would help alleviate those feelings. However, she developed complications and had to spend her last six months in bed. She and her husband felt a lot of strain because of this inconvenience. Yet she was certain that the birth of this baby would clear up the emptiness she had been feeling prior to her pregnancy. Margaret is devastated by the death of her child and can't understand why God has done this to her. Given the message of "The Cross and the Crown," how could Margaret work with this situation?

QUESTIONS FOR GROUP DISCUSSION

Organized according to sections within the chapter

Introduction

1. The way of the cross is described as "taking a definite stand" on this statement, "For I am determined not to know anything among you, save Jesus Christ, and Him crucified." Try to rephrase this statement in universal terms.

2. Do you feel that the cross represents something very definite in each person's life? In what way?

Why Is It Necessary to Bear a Cross?
Because One Was Borne by Another?

3. Do you agree that all crosses are of your own making? Can another person with free will impose crosses on you?

4. What does the text mean by "the delusion of the senses"?

5. Do you think we can help someone else overcome an obstacle if we haven't conquered the same condition in our own life? Why or why not?

6. In your opinion, how is it possible that "We never lose so long as we give"?

Why Was It Necessary
That He, the Maker of Heaven and Earth,
Should Bear a Cross?

7. Is it possible to be a "follower of Christ" without being a Christian?

8. According to this section, Christ showed us "how it was possible to live a perfect, blameless life with all the disintegrating influences that surround us day by day." Do you really think it's possible to live a perfect life?

9. What is the difference between "sons [children] of men" and "sons [children] of God"?

10. Ponder this line from John 15: "Greater love hath no man than this, that a man lay down his life for his friends." What does this mean?

Why Did He Come into the World as a Man
That He Might Bear a Cross?

11. "The Word came and dwelt among men, the offspring of self in a material world. The Word overcame the world..." Can you explain this?

Why Do We, as Individuals, Necessarily Bear Much That He Bore, and Yet Say That When Taking His Yoke upon Us the Cross Becomes Easy?

12. How can bearing a difficult cross lead you to a deeper understanding of love and forgiveness?
13. Can you explain how "matter is a tool with which to shape the nobler life"?

Does the Life Lived According to Our Own Faith, Our Own Understanding, and Our Own Walking in His Presence Explain Why Each Soul Must Bear a Cross?

14. What do you think it means to have an "ideal set in Him"?
15. How can material concerns get in the way of your relationship with God? How might you reconcile this conflict?

Why Has the Cross Been Chosen Rather Than Some Other Philosophy That Might Correlate the Material and Spiritual Life?

16. Do you think this section satisfactorily answers the question of why the cross is a symbol of spiritual attainment? Why or why not?
17. Can you explain the difference between "Jesus the man" and "Jesus the Christ" as they're used in this section?
18. Explain the difference between "becoming the way" and "pointing the way."

Why Is the Cross the Emblem of Shame, Necessary for Those Who Seek the Crown?

19. Have you ever experienced what you could describe as "the crown"? For example: the joy of completing a work or the reward of a finished race. Did you have to carry a cross to get it?
20. How has this chapter helped you understand more clearly your purpose for this life?

Why Must I, as a Soul in a Material Plane, Bear a Cross?

21. Do you agree with the statement in this section that says we are "entering the greatest test period in the history of the world"? If so, what can you do to help?
22. This section promises that as we meet our crosses and overcome our temptations, we become heirs to the "crown of glory." How would you describe this "crown of glory"?
23. How could our lives change as we begin to recognize that our purpose in life is to "be one with the Father"?

SUGGESTED SUPPLEMENTAL READING

1. *Experiments in a Search for God,* "The Cross and the Crown"
2. *Library Series,* Volume 16, *Expanded Search for God,* "The Cross and the Crown"
3. *Library Series,* Volume 7, *Study Group Readings,* 262-35 — 262-39
4. Circulating Files: #050 Jesus the Pattern and You
                               #052 Karma and the Law of Grace
                               #142 Stepping-Stones Not Stumbling Blocks

5. Suggested Bible Verses: Job
                               Psalm 22
                               Malachi 4:1-3
                               Luke 11:9-10
                               Luke 15:11-32
                               John 3:16-20
                               John 12:23-27
                               Acts 4:10-12
                               Romans 8:28-39
                               James 1:12-27

The Lord Thy God Is One

THINGS TO DO

Choose one of the following and try it for a week:

1. Spend a week looking for evidence of the oneness of God. Look both "within" through meditation or dreams, as well as "without" in your observation of nature and other people.
2. We are promised that we can awaken to Oneness through exercising the "fruits of the spirit." Not through "some great vision, but just being kind and performing each task cheerfully." Choose one day when you make an effort to perform each task, no matter how mundane, in a "kind and cheerful manner." Does this help awaken in you a sense of God's oneness?
3. Make a special effort for a week to recognize and appreciate other people's contribution to your day (and the Oneness of God's work). Find a way to express your appreciation for the services done by others. This may simply be a kind word or a friendly smile. Honor in your heart the "niche" that they fill.
4. We are told that we awaken to the Oneness of God by keeping our minds "in constant touch with and filled with that which is stimulating and uplifting." For a week, try to keep your mind focused on positive things. Select material to read and

TV programs to watch which are uplifting and positive. Keep in your own mind thoughts of hope and appreciation.

5. This chapter compares the influence of our thoughts on others to the ripples of water radiating from a dropped pebble. Practice for one week having only positive thoughts and feelings about one particular person in your life.

6. Jesus promises that we can have a personal relationship with our Creator. For one week invite God's presence into your daily activities. Then act with the expectancy that He will guide your thoughts and actions.

7. Take time this week to study a particular culture, people, or "movement" with which you don't currently agree. Study the causes, needs, and purposes and see if you can realize any areas of agreement and harmony.

8. Spend a week trying to apply this line from the text: "Strive to see God in every one as well as in every thing." Make a special effort to recognize that God is operating through others as well as yourself.

9. Remember that wherever you are, in whatever you're given to do, you are filling a vital "niche in the great Oneness."

THINGS TO THINK

1. Looking back over my life, where have I seen evidence of God working through others?

2. Ponder this: "God's power is manifesting in and through me in my every act, word, and deed."

3. This chapter says, " . . . our acts, whether good or bad, affect others. As in our bodies, when a member is injured, the whole suffers, so do we as individuals influence the whole of society." Can I think of any times when my actions may have had a beneficial or positive effect on another individual or society in general? Any negative incidents?

4. What are the ways that I can show by practical application that I am a "worker with God"? Where in the past have I seen this demonstrated in my life?

5. How might my current life's activities be standing in the way of experiencing oneness with God?

6. How sincere is my desire to realize that "the Lord our God is One"?

7. Have I ever given serious thought to the idea that the people

of the earth are one great family and that what affects someone on the other side of the world affects me?

8. What can I do to fulfill better my own special niche in life?
9. Do I separate my life and activities into different compart-
ments and feel that meditation time and Study Group meetings or church are more spiritual times than cleaning the
house, driving in traffic, or earning my paycheck?

THINGS TO PONDER

1. Janet works eight hours a day in an accounting department.
Mornings and evenings she's busy attending to her young
children. By 8:00 p.m. she wants to collapse on the couch and
watch TV. A member of her Study Group has told her that her
mind "should be in constant touch with and filled with that
which is stimulating and uplifting." How might she respond to
this comment?

2. Marjorie is in a Study Group and has just finished reading
"The Lord Thy God Is One." She's trying to "see God in every
one and every thing." At times she gets a glimmer of this
awareness and the joy it brings. But invariably, she then runs
into a situation which drives this awareness out of her head.
Her husband will complain about her cooking, or her children
will begin to fight and scream at each other, or a driver will cut
in front of her and almost cause an accident. Marjorie wants
to see God everywhere, but at times like these it just seems so
unreal. What can she do?

3. John (your brother-in-law) is very interested in two subjects:
religion and world affairs. He is a very devoted Christian and
feels fortunate to belong to the "true religion." John feels it is
a Christian duty to bring the world to the "One True God."
Otherwise, thousands of souls will be eternally damned. He
can't understand why God allows false religions to continue
and wonders if He wants Christians to launch a new crusade.
You know that John will raise this issue with you at an upcoming family reunion. How will you respond?

4. Larry has trouble relating to this chapter. He tells his group
that when he sees all the turmoil in the world and all the
suffering, he can't understand how anyone could see these as
manifestations of a loving God. What would you say to him if
you were in his group?

5. Mike has always prided himself on the great relationship he has with his son, Matthew. They seem to be connected on many levels. He had quite a shock last week when Matthew, who is 15 years old, informed him that he has decided to go and live with his mother for a while. Since she lives more than a thousand miles away, Mike is having a hard time dealing with the situation. He wants to be understanding of his son's needs and wishes in the matter, but now he feels as if his connecting link with Matthew has been broken. How can Mike use the concept of oneness to help him in this situation?

QUESTIONS FOR GROUP DISCUSSION

Organized according to sections within the chapter

Introduction

1. Why is unity such a different concept to realize and manifest?
2. Can success, money, or power become a god? Can you think of other less obvious concerns, such as "to be well thought of," that we might set up as gods?

The Manifestations of God Are One

3. We are told that "The people of the earth are one great family. We should love without distinction, knowing that God is in all." What would it take to make this happen?
4. How can *everything* that is in the universe—the beautiful, the ugly, the good, the evil—all be manifestations of the Oneness of God?
5. If "God is One" then why are there so many different religions?

How We May Come into the Realization of the Oneness

6. What is the lesson that nature teaches and how is it taught?
7. In your opinion, what is the meaning of the line, " . . . all material things are, in essence, spiritual"?
8. What are some of the things that individuals can do to become conscious of Oneness?

The At-Onement Through Jesus, the Christ

9. How can recognizing "the Oneness of Creative Force" make us truly free?
10. How did Jesus demonstrate his consciousness of "the Oneness of Creative Force"?

11. The text says, "He was ever explaining and demonstrating the truths which He knew would make men free." Which of these is especially meaningful to you? Why?

Personal Experiences

12. What evidence have you seen that seems to confirm the existence of Oneness in the universe?

Conclusion

13. If we are to understand Oneness, "We must believe that He is, and that He rewards those who seek to do His will." How does He reward us? What can we expect as rewards?

SUGGESTED SUPPLEMENTAL READING

1. *Experiments in a Search for God,* "The Lord Thy God Is One"
2. *Library Series,* Volume 16, *Expanded Search for God,* "The Lord Thy God Is One"
3. *Library Series,* Volume 7, *Study Group Readings,* 262-40 — 262-43
4. Circulating Files: #012 Christ Consciousness
   #077 The Meaning of "The Lord Thy God Is One"
5. Suggested Bible Verses: Deuteronomy 6 & 30
   Psalm 23
   Matthew 25:31-46
   Mark 12:28-33
   John 14-17
   I Corinthians 12
   Colossians 3:12-17

Love

THINGS TO DO

Choose one of the following and try it for a week:

1. During the week, try to really *feel* delight and joy in the company of others.
2. For one week, use a portion of your meditation to focus on the love that God has *for you!* Try to abide in that love throughout the day.
3. Seek to find examples of love in your surroundings that you just haven't taken the time to notice before.
4. Focus for several days on trying to make choices that you feel are prompted by unselfish love for others.
5. This week, make a special effort to express kindness to others, particularly those with whom you now have difficulties.
6. Is there a situation in your life that you are having trouble with or some necessary task that you don't enjoy doing? Maybe it's something small, like balancing your checkbook or filing paperwork at your job. Maybe it's a bigger condition—a relationship or a job you dislike. Examine the item and find *one* aspect—only one—that you can truly say you love about it and watch what happens to this condition. It does not matter how small the one aspect is; just be certain you can honestly say, "I love this part of it."

7. Try for a day to "give out the best that is in you" in every interaction with another during that day.

8. Complain about nothing for one day—not the weather, food service, someone smoking, another driver, a task assigned, a co-worker, your spouse, friend, or child... not one complaint.

9. For one week strive to see only good in all.

10. Be aware of occasions during the week when you feel out of harmony with your environment. At those times, take a few moments to appreciate the world around you (the fresh air, another person, a beautiful song on the radio) and give thanks for your life.

11. We're told in this chapter, "He that does not love his worst enemy has not even begun to develop." Think of someone (living or dead) whom you might consider an "enemy." Every day for a week pray for help in loving that person.

12. For at least one day, try not to think or speak any unkind thought or word about any individual (including yourself).

THINGS TO THINK

1. Ponder the following line from the text: "The power of love is unlimited."

2. Remember, "Loving those who are imperfect is no more than what God does for me."

3. What situations in my life might be separating me from the "love of God"?

4. Ponder this line: "Love never dies; it is eternal."

5. Do I ever feel that I'm being guided and protected by guardian angels?

6. Are there areas in my life where I'm limiting the power of love?

7. Are there any difficult situations or conditions in your life where you can apply this thought: "Since God wants me to overcome this hardship, the means will be provided"?

8. Can I remember an experience from my past which I thought was a problem but now recognize as a blessing?

9. Reflect on this passage from the text: "Love is God. The whole law is fulfilled in these three words."

10. Am I ready to accept that true love has no place for hate? Does hate still lodge somewhere in my heart?

11. Every one of my thoughts—both loving and unloving—are

constantly molding the situations, activities, and even other people in my life.

12. In most of my relationships with others, do I offer my love to them unselfishly or does my love frequently expect something in return?

THINGS TO FIGURE OUT

1. Jerry believes in the power of love. He has found that usually, when you show kindness to others, you receive kindness in return. He treats others as kindly as possible. He has just been told what a "friend" recently said about him: "Don't be fooled by Jerry. He just puts on that 'nice guy' act so he can get what he wants." This shocked Jerry. He wonders if there's any truth to it. At the same time, he now feels self-conscious when he's around the person who made the remark. What insights from the chapter on "Love" might help Jerry deal with this situation?

2. Bridget is beginning to feel a bit manipulated by her teenage daughter, Connie. In most respects, Connie is a wonderful child. However, more and more whenever she wants to do something that her mother is against, Connie has been using the line, "If you love me, you'll let me." Mostly these have been small things like staying out extra late at a friend's party or borrowing the car more frequently than Bridget thinks is wise. To make matters worse, whenever Connie is depressed she often says, "No one loves me." How can Bridget make it clear that Connie is indeed loved while at the same time avoid her manipulation?

3. Jennifer frequently talks to her next-door neighbor, Sue, about the love and fellowship that is present in her Study Group and how much more loving she herself has become as a result of her participation. Sue has observed, however, that Jennifer is critical of associates at work and often complains about how she is not treated as favorably as another. She feels there is something inconsistent in Jennifer's understanding of love and fellowship. Sue wonders what she should do.

4. Bob has always tried to be loving. However, he finds that people seem to take advantage of him. More and more Bob finds that he is bitter about what is happening. He knows that he must change something in himself to bring about a change

in his life. If you were Bob, what would you do?

5. Kathy and Liz have been friends for many years and are now attending college together. Liz is a brilliant student who can get by with doing very little studying, while Kathy must put a lot of time and effort into her school work. On several occasions Liz has helped Kathy meet her homework deadlines. Now, Kathy has started to expect Liz's help whenever she feels pressured for time. Liz and Kathy want to attend a big party on Saturday night, but there is a particularly difficult paper due on Monday. Liz knows that Kathy won't be able to go unless Liz does the paper for her. Kathy says that if Liz is really her friend she'll help her out of this bind. How can Liz express love in this situation?

QUESTIONS FOR GROUP DISCUSSION

Organized according to sections within the chapter

Introduction

1. Why is the whole law fulfilled in "love is God"?
2. Where have you seen divine love manifested today?

Love Manifested

3. How do we commune with God in nature?
4. Can you think of someone who demonstrates the kind of love that brings "joy through service even in toil and pain"?

The Power of Love

5. How can we "see only goodness and purity in everybody and everything" and still discern right from wrong?
6. We're told to "lay down our lives for others." How can you apply this ideal without actually taking it literally?
7. What does love have to do with abundance—materially and spiritually?

The Test of Love

8. Why is it insufficient to love only those who love us? Why must we love strangers? enemies?
9. How can love prevent us from being disappointed in things, people, conditions?

Love Is Giving

10. How does the law of love make other laws more effective? For example, the law of recompense, the law of love, the law

of earth forces?

11. How do you differentiate between like and love? Between love and passion? Between being "in love" and divine love?

12. How is the power of true love eternal?

Divine Love Passes Understanding

13. Why does everyone have trouble accepting the "love that passes understanding"?

Personal Experiences

14. Discuss this line from the text: "Herein is love, not that we loved God, but that He loved us."

Conclusion

15. What is meant by "the day of the Lord is near at hand"?

SUGGESTED SUPPLEMENTAL READING

1. *Experiments in a Search for God,* "Love"
2. *Library Series,* Volume 16, *Expanded Search for God,* "Love"
3. *Library Series,* Volume 7, *Study Group Readings,* 262-44 — 262-49
4. Circulating Files: #017 Creative Forces: Essence of Life
    #074 Love and Spirituality
    #137 Fruits of the Spirit
    #149 If You Call, I Will Hear
5. Suggested Bible Verses: Psalm 91
    Matthew 5:43-48
    Matthew 6:24-33
    Mark 12:28-34
    Luke 10:26-37
    John 3:16-21
    John 14-17
    I Corinthians 13
    Romans 8:31-39
    I John 4:7-21
    I John 5:1-5

PART II

Answers
to Questions
You May Have

WHAT TO DO FOR YOUR GROUP'S FIRST MEETING

You have each come together to share in a very special group experience. Here are some suggestions on how to conduct your first meeting.

1. *Get Acquainted*

   Have each person tell a little about himself or herself and how he/she got interested in the Edgar Cayce information. The host or hostess may also want to tell how he/she decided to have this first meeting and how the Study Group Department at Virginia Beach helped.

2. *Introduction*

   Pass copies of *A Search for God,* Book I, and the handbook around the group. Read together pages 3-5 of the handbook so each will be familiar with how the Study Group program began and how this handbook can help.

3. *Affirmation*

   Read together the section in Part II of the handbook entitled "Affirmations" (page 78). Then turn to the "Cooperation" chapter and read the affirmation found at the beginning. Discuss its possible meaning. It is not necessary for all to agree or to feel it is completely understood. Agree to set aside 10 to 15 minutes daily for a meditation period during the next week using the affirmation as a focus. Although meditation procedures are outlined on pages 79-86 of this handbook, you might also want to take time during the week to read the meditation information at the beginning of *A Search for God.*

4. *Disciplines and Application*

   Read together pages 77-78 of this handbook entitled "Disciplines and Application." Then turn to page 11 of the handbook entitled "Cooperation." Read through the suggested "Things to Do." Select one you will try this week.

5. *Planning Your Next Meeting*

   Decide what time and where to meet. Most groups meet weekly at the same location. Some groups choose to change locations from time to time. Leadership is shared in *A Search for God* groups. Group leaders begin the meeting, facilitate the discussions, and conduct the meditation. Everyone in the group should take a turn at leading a meeting. It is important to rotate leaders to avoid dependence upon one individual. Some groups select a different leader for each chapter; however, many groups change leadership every week. Still others find that having the leader serve for a three-week period is more comfortable. Decide now who will be next week's leader for your group. When the group meets again, you'll want to use the "Suggested Meeting Format" found on page 6 of this handbook, and start with the "Cooperation" chapter of *A Search for God*.

TIMETABLES FOR GROUP STUDY

New groups often ask how long it should take to go through a single lesson. There is no fixed answer to this question. The group must set its own speed. Your group will find that some chapters move faster than others. Also, different times of year seem to affect the rate of progress. You're encouraged to find the rate of study that *feels best* for your particular group. However, if you'd like more specific guidance, here are a few options:

1. You can set whatever time limit you choose or not set any limit at all. Most groups just proceed through the material at whatever pace feels comfortable. Some groups may spend five or six weeks on a chapter; some more, some less. You needn't be concerned with pace or time limits unless your group chooses to do so.

2. Do one lesson in a month. This speed is faster than the usual rate. Your group will need discipline to keep up the pace. With this speed, you'll finish the program *(A Search for God,* Books I and II) in two years.

3. Try going through an entire lesson in a single meeting. This is a *very* challenging speed. This works best, of course, if each member reads the lesson before the meeting. If you persevere at this speed you can finish the entire program in 25 weeks or six months. Many experienced groups who have been through the books a couple of times find this helpful. It's not recommended for new groups.

There are 24 lessons in the *Search for God* program, not counting the "Meditation" section. The first 12 are contained in Book I, while the second 12 are in Book II. You should keep in mind that setting a beginning and an ending date to a Study Group experience is perfectly okay. While the program was originally designed to be continuous, a new group may decide to limit the experience to only six months or a year. It is possible to complete the program in that time and it is a legitimate option for a group. Naturally, each group has the right and power to choose for itself.

Upon completing the last lesson in Book II, groups traditionally review the "Meditation" section and then begin again with lesson number one. People who have been through the program several times are surprised at finding new insights into the material each time they read it.

THE LANGUAGE USED IN A *SEARCH FOR GOD*

The traditional language used in the *A Search for God* material sometimes presents an obstacle to students. Passages from the Bible are quoted and paraphrased throughout the books. They also refer to God in the traditional masculine gender. Because Edgar Cayce was a devoted student of the King James Version of the Bible, this book had a clear influence on the language used in his psychic readings. Please feel free to interpret the language in a form that is suitable to your own understanding. Remember, it is the meaning carried by the language which is important and not the language itself.

A DEFINITION OF THE CHRIST

There are frequent references to the Christ throughout the text. Finding them, many people wonder if this material is limited to Christians. However, the *Search for God* material is meant to be universal. It honors all religions and individuals.

The Christ Consciousness was described in the readings as the awareness *within every soul* of its oneness with God, which is imprinted as a pattern on the *mind,* and waiting to be awakened by the *will.*

Therefore, simply put, the Christ Consciousness is the individual awareness of our oneness with God.

DISCIPLINES AND APPLICATION

Try living the precepts in these chapters. You only learn by application and experience. The Edgar Cayce readings strongly caution against seeking spiritual knowledge without steadily applying what you learn in your daily relationships and activities. On the other hand, they promise that if you *do* apply these spiritual principles in your daily living, they can help make your life more worthwhile in every way. It's not enough just to know spiritual law intellectually. *Applying* the law leads to growth. In fact, knowledge not applied creates obstacles to your own soul development.

Some new groups find it confusing at first to take this step from reading and discussion to real application. This is why the booklet includes a "Things to Do" section for every chapter. This section provides you with specific and practical ways to use the spiritual laws you're reading about and discussing in each lesson.

Think of yourself as a spiritual researcher, putting to the test newly discovered laws and seeing how they make a difference in your daily routine. "Experiment" is an excellent word for this part of your journey. It's important to approach these weekly applications with an attitude of adventure.

Then at the group meeting, you can share with the other members the results of your experiment. Listen to the other reports. This testing and sharing transforms Study Groups into spiritual laboratories.

AFFIRMATIONS

At the beginning of each lesson in *A Search for God,* there is an affirmation which was given in the Edgar Cayce reading for that chapter. Each affirmation was specifically designed to be used with that lesson and serves two principal purposes in your study: as a meditation tool and as a way to deepen your understanding of the chapter.

You're encouraged to use the affirmation as a tool for more effective meditating. The readings recommend memorizing the affirmation and using it to reach a quiet meditative state. Begin by repeating it first aloud and then silently to yourself as you begin to meditate. The affirmation helps quiet your mind and allows you to focus on the presence of the Divine.

The silent repetition of the words leads eventually to a state of mind which might be described as "attentive stillness." Once you feel yourself in this state, stop repeating the words and instead experience the "spirit" or "essence" of them. If your mind begins to wander, which is normal, simply resume saying the words to yourself as before until you again reach that state of "attentive stillness."

You'll find that some affirmations are easier to memorize than others. Some of the wording may seem unusual. If you simply can't manage to commit one to memory, picking a small portion of it is an effective way to begin.

The affirmation also summarizes the precepts or spiritual laws that are presented in the chapter you are studying. Therefore, a provocative discussion question would be, "How does the affirmation illustrate this lesson?"

These affirmations build upon one another. They are verses which capture the entire chapter and lead to a personal spiritual experience.

PRAYER AND MEDITATION

Some people are not sure of the difference between prayer and meditation. A simple way of defining the two is comparing them to everyday conversation. A conversation has two parts—talking and listening. In order to really communicate, you have to do both. Communication with the Creator is the same way. You can think of prayer as talking to God, while meditation is like listening. It is quieting your mind and focusing on the presence of the Divine. The Cayce readings tell us that we spiritualize our minds and even our bodies during meditation. Because our minds build what we dwell upon, positive changes actually take place within us. As we try to become aware of the Spirit of the Creator, we're given energy and power to further our spiritual journey.

A MEDITATION PROCEDURE

Meditation is not merely a 15- or 20-minute discipline done each day. It is an entire life style, because the way in which we live our lives deeply influences the experiences we have in the formal meditation session. Our ideals and purposes have an effect, the same as what we eat or read or think about during the day.

For purposes of this outline, however, let's assume that you are consciously working or doing the best that you can with these ongoing influences. What steps can you, as a seeker, follow in order to meditate according to the Cayce readings? These steps have proven to be successful for thousands of people.

1. Set a regular time of day for your meditation session. The regularity makes it more likely you will remember to meditate, plus you may find it easier to get your mind more quickly

focused and quiet if you have such a consistent time of day. Choose the time when you are most likely to be alert, least distracted, and most able to keep focused on your spiritual aspirations and ideals.

At first you may want to have relatively brief meditation sessions—perhaps only three or four minutes of an actual silence period. Later, you can expand this period to 10, 15, or 20 minutes. Sample meditation postures are shown on page 85.

2. Choose from among the many aids for attunement which may help create the right mood for you and which assist you in getting yourself focused on your spiritual aspirations. There is no set regimen for this step. Pick from among these or other exercises which you may find useful.

> (a) Reading from the Bible or some other spiritual literature
> (b) Conscious, focused breathing (see page 83) and a breathing exercise (see page 84)
> (c) Head and neck exercise (see page 82)
> (d) Chanting
> (e) Using incense
> (f) Listening to inspirational music or quieting, centering music

3. Pray. Take at least two or three minutes to attune your mind through prayer. You may want to use the Lord's Prayer or another prayer which you say silently (or aloud) as a spontaneous expression of your feelings. There are many forms of prayer—petition, praise, thanksgiving, forgiveness, etc. Choose each day what seems most appropriate.

4. Repeat several times the affirmation you have chosen for meditation. If you wish, you may start with saying it aloud, but then move to a silent repetition in your mind.

For example, in each lesson of *A Search for God* the Cayce readings offered a specific meditation affirmation keyed to the concepts of that spiritual growth step. Having memorized the appropriate affirmation, you will silently repeat it in your mind. If the entire affirmation seems too lengthy, begin with only a part of it that is most meaningful to you.

Real meditating begins when you start *feeling the meaning* of the words, rather than just saying them mechanically. Start to sense the spirit which the words of the affirmation represent.

When you begin to feel this inner meaning, then stop repeating the words and *silently hold in your attention* this spirit, this feeling. If, after 10 or 20 or 30 seconds, you discover that your attention has been distracted, don't despair. This happens to virtually all meditators. Gently bring your attention back by silently repeating the affirmation one or more times. Then, when you once more feel the meaning and spirit behind the words, let go of the affirmation and just hold that feeling in *silence.*

Most likely you will have to return to the words of the affirmation many times in a single meditation session. Your mind is accustomed to darting from one distraction to another. Don't be discouraged. Despite the frequency with which distractions may arise (internally or externally), there are still great positive effects produced in your body and mind by meditation.

5. At the end of this time of using the affirmation and trying to be silent, take another period for prayer. This time, however, use a very specific form of prayer. For several minutes pray for *others.*

If there are people who have specifically asked for your prayers in healing or for changing a condition, then it is fine to pray for that. Otherwise, pray for people for whom you have concern by blessing them and surrounding them with light. It's always good to add "God's will be done."

Here are some simple exercises which may help you prepare for meditation.

Head and Neck
Exercises

The head and neck exercise is designed to relax the
muscles around your neck and shoulder.

Note: All head and neck exercises should be done slowly and gently, without straining or
forcing the muscles.

1.

Sit in an upright
position.

Tip head forward,
trying to touch
chin to chest.

Return head to
upright position.

Repeat
three
times.

2.

Sit in an upright
position.

Tip head back-
ward, as if to look
at ceiling.

Return head to
upright position.

Repeat
three
times.

3.

Sit in upright
position.

Tip head toward
right shoulder, as
if to touch right
ear to shoulder.

Incorrect:
Shoulder should
not lift or shrug.

Return to upright
position.

Repeat three
times to right;
three times to left.

Sit in upright
position.

Drop head
forward,
touching chin
to chest.

Rotate head
gently in a
clockwise
direction.

Repeat three times clockwise,
three times counterclockwise.

Three-Stage
Focused Breathing

The breathing exercises are recommended for
balancing the energies of the body.

Filling the Lungs:

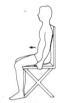  

Stage 1: Fill bottom of
lungs, abdomen
expands.

Stage 2: Fill middle
third of lungs, chest
cavity expands.

Stage 3: Fill top third of
lungs, shoulders come
up.

Emptying the Lungs:

Stage 1: Top third of
lungs empties first,
shoulders relax.

Stage 2: Chest cavity
contracts, pushing air
out of middle third of
lungs.

Stage 3: Abdomen is
pulled in, forcing all
remaining air out of
lungs.

Breathing Exercise

1.

Air

Left nostril is held
closed, air is drawn in
through right nostril.

Air is exhaled through
mouth.

Repeat three times,
using the three-stage
focused breathing.

2.

Air

Right nostril is held
closed, air is drawn in
through left nostril.

Left nostril is held
closed, air is exhaled
through right nostril.

Repeat three times,
using the three-stage
focused breathing.

Postures for Meditation

The meditation positions are suggested in the Cayce readings for comfort and stability. You should use the position which feels best for you.

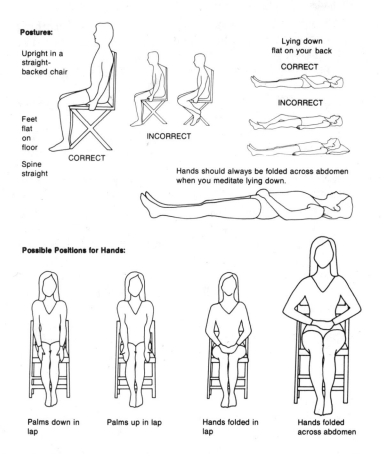

Postures:

Upright in a straight-backed chair

Feet flat on floor

Spine straight

CORRECT

INCORRECT

Lying down flat on your back

CORRECT

INCORRECT

Hands should always be folded across abdomen when you meditate lying down.

Possible Positions for Hands:

Palms down in lap

Palms up in lap

Hands folded in lap

Hands folded across abdomen

PART II
86

WHEN YOU MEDITATE AS A GROUP

When your Study Group meditates together, it's helpful if you choose a member to lead it. This person begins and ends the meditation period, leading the opening and closing prayers. Here is a suggested outline:

1. Allow time for the head and neck exercises and breathing exercises. People who want to use these can proceed at their own pace.
2. Most groups start with a short prayer. Some use the Lord's Prayer.
3. Say the affirmation aloud or have the group say it together two or three times.
4. Allow ten to fifteen minutes of silence during which the members hold their attention on the essence of the affirmation.
5. At the end of this period the leader says a prayer asking for the group to be used as channels of blessing and healing for those whose names are either called aloud or brought to mind.
6. Close the meditation period with a prayer or the affirmation. Many groups recite together the 23rd Psalm.

One way to make your individual daily meditation more powerful is to pick a time each day when the whole Study Group can meditate together. You don't have to be in one place to share a meditation. It may be hard to find a time when everyone is available, but it's worth trying to select such a moment even if just a portion of the group is able to manage it.

DREAM STUDY

Often one of the first places you'll see evidence of soul growth is in your dreams. The Edgar Cayce readings encourage dream study, describing dreams as a potential source of spiritual guidance. Dreams can be an enriching personal experience even if you choose not to discuss them in a group setting. However, many Study Groups do include a time for discussing dreams.

Although you are encouraged to work with dreams in your group, you should be aware of some problems that may arise.

One of these is keeping dream discussions reasonably short. Most people find dreams so very interesting that dream study can easily take over the entire meeting! Here are three ways to include dream study without letting the length of time get out of hand.

1. Schedule time before or after the regular meeting.
2. Discuss only one dream during the regular meeting, and limit your discussion time to five or ten minutes. You don't have to get final closure on the dream's meaning for the discussion to be helpful.
3. Reserve a special meeting for discussing dreams. This might be a different one altogether or a special occasion on the regular meeting night.

Another challenge when working with dreams is simply learning how to interpret them. While there is a lot of information in the Edgar Cayce readings on how to interpret dreams, the *A Search for God* material does not address this subject. However, several excellent books are available from A.R.E. which can teach you how to work with dreams. Here are a few:

1. *How to Interpret Your Dreams*, by Mark Thurston
2. *Dreams: Tonight's Answers for Tomorrow's Questions*, by Mark Thurston
3. *Dreams—Your Magic Mirror*, by Elsie Sechrist
4. *Edgar Cayce on Dreams*, by Harmon Bro
5. A.R.E. audiotaped courses on dream interpretation:
   "How to Understand and Interpret Your Dreams"
   "Dream Interpretation Made Easy"

It's important to remember that dreams are helping you on many levels even if you don't always remember them or understand what they mean.

WHEN IT'S YOUR TURN TO LEAD THE GROUP MEETING

You'll want to review the "Suggested Meeting Format" on page 6. You may also want to look over the handbook's "Questions for Discussion" on the chapter your group is studying.

Since you'll be leading the closing meditation, you might want to look over "When You Meditate as a Group" on page 86.

HOW YOUR GROUP CAN HELP ITSELF

This section will touch on some of the most common situations that can arise in small group activities. Some of these challenges involve the entire group while others relate more to your own personal experiences.

It's important to remember that keys to healthy group dynamics extend beyond the two-hour weekly meeting. Over time you will be building close personal relationships with the other members of your group. Just taking time every day to pray for each group member by name has a profound effect on these developing relationships. The Edgar Cayce readings gave this shared moment of prayer the highest priority for Study Groups. Try setting a time every day when all the group members can meditate and pray together, wherever they may be. You'll find that the group experience continues through the week even when you're not together.

As the group experience unfolds, you will find that, as with all relationships, various difficulties may arise. Here are some of the challenges you may encounter in your Study Group:

MONOPOLIZING THE CONVERSATION

Almost invariably there will be some people who are more comfortable than others in speaking out during group discussion. This is natural. It's all right for some members to talk more than others. However, a central challenge to successful group involvement is creating a well-balanced flow of discusson. This might be called "tossing the ball." Mastering this balance is particularly important during the early stages of a group's development. You may find that one or two individuals begin to dominate the group discussion. This can become a source of considerable frustration. If allowed to go unchecked, it can drive members away and even lead to the total breakup of the group itself. Since this situation often surfaces when a group is new and unsure of itself, it's important to address this issue before it gets out of hand.

A good way to handle this situation is for the assigned leader to take a firm hand in balancing the flow of discussion. He or she can do this by setting down some simple operational rules in the beginning. One possible rule is to ask members to raise their hand if they want to talk. The leader can then direct a question to another group member even if the person monopolizing the conversation still has more to say. Some groups have found that even more unusual methods are needed. For instance, one group decided to bring in a three-minute-egg timer. Each person's turn to talk could last only that long. In addition to the time limiter some groups have found it necessary to ring a bell when the time is up. This makes it very clear when one's turn is over.

Measures such as these are usually temporary. Most often the group quickly learns the courtesy of taking turns and group discussion begins to flow smoothly.

NON-PARTICIPATION

It's easy to overlook the non-participator. This is the person who attends the group meetings but who remains totally uninvolved in the discussions. The temptation in this situation is to ignore it. Yet this person may have much to offer in ideas and quiet energy. However, due to shyness or insecurity these gifts are not easily offered. The action in this case would be to gently encourage the individual to join in more fully with the group process. There are several ways that the members of the group can help. One obvious way is to pose questions to the person during the meeting. Those that draw on the person's own experience will probably be most successful. For example: "Can you remember any time during the week when you felt the spirit of cooperation at work?"

Another way to draw out a non-participating person is to find out his or her special interests and then refer to these subjects in questions or in private conversation. For example, if a person has a special interest in cars, you might ask questions that refer to them. For example: "How does a car demonstrate cooperation in action?"

Another way to draw out a non-participator is to arrange some non-group social time, such as visiting on the phone or having lunch. Often a person who is shy in a group setting will feel more comfortable in a less public atmosphere. As the person grows more comfortable with individual group members, he or she will naturally begin participating more in the group.

Be careful not to embarrass people by trying too hard to draw them out. People need time to open up.

TIMES WHEN YOU EXPERIENCE DRY PERIODS

On any journey there are times when you get tired and lose interest. This is equally true of a spiritual journey. During a Study Group's life, every member will experience occasional periods of frustration and even doubt. In addition, the group as a whole will likely face this situation.

Both individually and as a group, you need to accept these dry periods as a natural part of growth. Once you learn to identify these stages, you can move through them more easily and put them behind you.

How can you tell when you're going through a personal dry spell? One symptom is a persistent disinterest in going to group meetings. Another is a sharp loss of inspiration in your reading. Material which had earlier filled you with wonder and excitement may suddenly seem dull and repetitious. Continually forgetting to meditate or apply the weekly discipline is another sure sign that the spiritual path has become tedious.

How can you move past this dry period and rediscover the enthusiasm you had? If your Study Group begins to feel uninspiring, try getting more involved in other activities. Often a new group experience is so exciting that it eclipses all your other interests and involvements. It's important, however, to balance even a very special activity with the rest of your life. Church, neighborhood, or civic involvements are just three possibilities.

Another means of re-inspiring yourself is to find a very specific way of helping someone else. Sometimes study becomes dry from too little application. Helping someone in need is suggested throughout the Cayce readings as the most effective way of overcoming any personal problem. Opportunities are everywhere. You might find a personal need, such as a family member or a friend or you may prefer to serve others through community programs such as soup kitchens or charity drives.

However, it's also important to take care of your own needs. One need that you might be overlooking is the need for rest and relaxation. Are you setting aside a special time every day to nurture yourself? These are necessary to a balanced life. Try reviewing your daily schedule. Make sure you're making room for rest and play as well as work.

Finally, if you continue to feel uninspired and restless in your group study, you might try taking a vacation from the group for a while. Sometimes you just need to step back from it and let your interest return in its own time. If you decide on such a move, be sure to think of it as a positive step.

TIMES WHEN THE WHOLE GROUP
EXPERIENCES DRY PERIODS

Dry periods are natural not only for individuals but also for the group itself. Signs that a group is feeling stale include frequent absences, petty personality conflicts among group members, and uninteresting discussions. Many of the steps which help move individuals through dry periods are also very effective for groups. Service projects, such as clothing drives or other charity involvement, can work wonders in generating enthusiasm for a group. Also, special outings can be very effective in lifting a group out of the doldrums. You might use a meeting night to have a potluck dinner, inviting family and friends. You might decide to go to a particular movie, attend a lecture, or invite visitors to attend your group meeting. Some groups have enjoyed visiting different religious services and then discussing the experience at later meetings.

While a dry period is not necessarily a good time for groups to go recruiting, new members are often effective in generating renewed enthusiasm. Many groups have discovered that new members appear just when they needed them. This is an example of how the universe will cooperate with a sincere effort.

Temporarily studying some alternative material is also effective in picking up the interest of a group. You might try studying the original Study Group readings, a book of the Bible such as Psalms, or the sacred writings of other religions.

Finally, you must remember that Study Groups have a life cycle just like everything else. Not only will individuals come and go, but groups themselves have a beginning and an ending. Study Groups don't last forever. There will come a day when your group will disband. It's important not to feel badly about this. It's natural. Although the group itself may come to an end, the growth and enrichment it has given will remain with you permanently. When the time is right, perhaps you will form a new Study Group or join an existing one as another chapter in your search for God.

WHAT TO EXPECT WHEN YOU VISIT A GROUP

To find out where *A Search for God* Study Groups are meeting in your area, simply call or write:

A.R.E. Study Group Department
P.O. Box 595
Virginia Beach, VA 23451
(804) 428-3588

The Study Group Department will give you names of local A.R.E. Representatives. These local representatives can inform you of the groups meeting nearest you. You'll simply want to contact the chairperson of that group and ask to visit.

You'll probably find that your group meets in a private home. This helps to keep the Study Group personal, friendly, and easygoing. There will be from two to twelve people gathered together. The meeting will last about two hours and will begin and end on time.

The atmosphere is informal. The group is expecting visitors, so you'll be welcome. For an idea of what you can expect to happen, see the meeting format on page 6.

During your first meeting you may prefer to listen. However, if you would like to ask a question or offer an insight, you're certainly free to do so. This is a vital part of the Study Group experience.

Following the group's closing meditation, you'll probably hear various group members engaged in personal conversations, since group members often become friends.

Although the group will surely thank you for visiting and invite you back, you won't feel any pressure to join the group permanently. That decision is entirely up to you.

Please feel free to visit as many groups as you like. There may be many which are near enough to you. You can visit them all if you wish before you decide on a particular one. Groups are like individuals; each is different. It's perfectly natural for you to feel more at home with some groups than others.

You might also want to consider starting a group of your own. Simply get in touch with the A.R.E. Study Group Department, who will help you every step of the way.

HOW A.R.E. CAN HELP YOUR GROUP

Once you've formed a new group, you'll want to send in your group affiliation form as soon as possible so that you can obtain support materials from the Study Group Department. You'll receive the quarterly newsletter *Guidelines,* which will give you suggestions for enriching your Study Group meetings. You'll receive workshop materials designed to enhance your search for God.

Affiliation with A.R.E. helps to keep you informed on A.R.E. events happening in your area and at Virginia Beach. As an affiliated group, you can be put in touch with newcomers who may visit your group, if you wish. You can also be put in touch with other Search for God groups in your area.

It is important for all groups to affiliate regardless of size. You'll find a form enclosed in this booklet. Once a year you'll be invited to re-affiliate. This helps A.R.E. keep your records current and allows the organization to serve you better. Please take a few minutes one meeting to complete the form.

A.R.E. MEMBERSHIP

In addition to affiliating the Study Group with A.R.E., individuals may wish to become A.R.E. members. This is the best way to become familiar with the wealth of information in the Edgar Cayce readings. Please contact A.R.E. for membership information.

HOW YOU CAN HELP A.R.E. HELP OTHERS

Many groups have a special basket or coffee can they pass around as a way of obtaining voluntary contributions. Traditionally, groups send half of this money as a quarterly donation to the A.R.E. Study Group Department in Virginia Beach. The donation helps support efforts to provide services and materials for Study Groups like yours throughout the world.

The group can then use the remainder of the funds however it sees fit. There are many possibilities. Study Groups have sponsored local Group Starting Sessions in which they introduce the *A Search for God* material to their local community. Many have purchased books to add to a local library. Others contribute to a favorite charity. Some occasionally spend this money on a special social activity like a potluck dinner.

THE A.R.E. TODAY:

The Association for Research and Enlightenment, Inc. (A.R.E.®), is a membership organization founded by Edgar Cayce in 1931.

● 14,145 Cayce readings, the largest body of documented psychic information anywhere in the world, are housed in the A.R.E. Library/Conference Center in Virginia Beach, Virginia. These readings have been indexed under 10,000 different topics and are open to the public.

● An attractive package of membership benefits is available for modest yearly dues. Benefits include: a bi-monthly magazine; lessons for home study; a lending library through the mail, which offers collections of the actual readings as well as one of the world's best parapsychological book collections; names of doctors or health care professionals in your area.

● As an organization on the leading edge in exciting new fields, A.R.E. presents a selection of publications and seminars by prominent authorities in the fields covered, exploring such areas as parapsychology, dreams, meditation, world religions, holistic health, reincarnation and life after death, and personal growth.

● The unique path to personal growth outlined in the Cayce readings is developed through a worldwide program of Study Groups. These informal groups meet weekly in private homes.

● A.R.E. maintains a visitors' center where a bookstore, exhibits, classes, a movie, and audiovisual presentations introduce inquirers to concepts from the Cayce readings.

● A.R.E. conducts research into the helpfulness of both the medical and nonmedical readings, often giving members the opportunity to participate in the studies.

For more information and a color brochure, write or phone:

A.R.E., P.O. Box 595
Virginia Beach, VA 23451, (804) 428-3588